IN HIS PRESENCE
Seven Visits to the
Blessed Sacrament

by Christine Haapala
Illustrations by Gustave Doré

Suffering Servant Scriptorium
Fairfax, VA
www.sufferingservant.com

**Dedicated to the Blessed Virgin Mary,
Queen of Heaven and Earth**

Special thanks to Father Michael Duesterhaus for all of his
encouragement and spiritual direction.

TABLE OF ILLUSTRATIONS

TABLE OF CONTENTS

FOREWORD

THROUGH THE NIGHT WITH CHRIST
Father Elias Carr, Society of St. Leopold

The celebrations of the Sacred Triduum — Holy Thursday, Good Friday and the Easter Vigil — are the most solemn of the liturgical cycle. No time in the year reaches the heights that these days do. While we celebrate in every Mass the Paschal Mystery, the Triduum allows the Church to linger over the events of the last days of Christ's earthly life and the beginning of the New Creation in the Resurrection.

Naturally the celebration of these holy days finds its perfect form in the Sacred Liturgy. Here Jesus, Our great High Priest, prays on behalf of His Mystical Body, of which He is the head, to His Father in the singular act of worship that is the Holy Eucharist. Instituted as a Sacrament at the Last Supper as the source of salvation and eternal life, it represents in words and gestures, in bread and wine, the self-offering of Jesus on the Cross.

But that is not all, for the Holy Eucharist not only makes present the Son's laying down His life for His friends, but also the Father's acceptance of this perfect act of the Son's love for His enemies, His love for us. The Resurrection completes the Sacred Triduum by proclaiming the Father's response to human hatred and sin, whereupon the Father again calls sinners to repentance by the offer of forgiveness. The Risen Lord greets the Apostles with peace and gives them the authority to forgive, as they themselves have been forgiven.

The Sacred Liturgy recounts this inconceivable story of God's forbearance and mercy and calls us to turn away from the death-dealing ways of sin and to return to the source of life. However the celebration of the Sacred Triduum is too awesome, too dense to understand unless we take time to ponder and consider it.

One tradition associated with the pondering of the mystery of the Sacred Triduum is the custom of visiting the altars of reposition on Holy Thursday. Through this practice, the faithful visit seven churches after the Mass of the Lord's Supper in which was remembered the great event in which Christ instituted the Holy Eucharist and the Catholic Priesthood. The faithful go together from church to church, retracing symbolically the path of the Apostles as they descended from Mount Zion to the Garden of Gethsemane. Each visit before the decorated tabernacle, where the Real Presence is encountered, permits a few moments to meditate on an aspect of the Paschal Mystery and through intercessionary prayer to give some comfort and support to all those tempted to feel abandoned by God in their hour of trial.

In 2000, a number of us began this practice at Holy Spirit Catholic Church in Annandale, Virginia, and it continues to this day. Let this practice come to you and your families and friends, whereby you make the evening of Holy Thursday a moment of retreat from the distractions of the world. Visit Our Lord in the Blessed Sacrament in the parishes nearby, going together in a spirit of fellowship and joy, strengthening one another on the way to Calvary, His and ours, so that we who have died with Him might rise with Him on the day of our Resurrection.

Author's Note

During the Year of the Eucharist, October 2004 through October 2005, three events influenced me to write this book of meditations. First, while reading Blessed Anne Catherine Emmerich's <u>Dolorous Passion of Our Lord Jesus Christ</u>, I was profoundly moved when I read that Jesus fell seven times as he climbed the hill to Calvary on the *Via Dolorosa*. This sharply intensifies the Stations of the Cross where Jesus falls but three times. Second, I participated in our parish's Seven Church Pilgrimage to Adoration Chapels on the evening of Holy Thursday. *(For details on this devotion, see Father Carr's Foreword, page vii)*. And, finally, a couple shared a story with me that they were disappointed that their parish priest would not lead the Chaplet of Divine Mercy on Divine Mercy Sunday. So for seven consecutive days they prayed before the Blessed Sacrament that this priest's heart would be drawn to the Divine Mercy and the Eucharist – and his heart was.

Seven in Sacred Scriptures can be an exact number or a proverbial representation for a very large number. In this books of meditations, I outlined Seven Visits to the Blessed Sacrament. This book can be used in one evening, such as, during the Holy Thursday Seven Church Pilgrimage. It can be used for seven consecutive days for a special prayer request. And, it can be used periodically, whenever you spend time visiting Jesus in the Blessed Sacrament.

This book of meditations is designed to support you as a guide during adoration – as a way to get started. Each visit focuses on one vice to eliminate and one virtue to perfect. *The just man falls seven times and rises again. … [V]irtuous paths are from the LORD. Prv 24:16, Sir 11:15.* In our spiritual journey, we are called to purge ourselves of the propensity toward the Seven Deadly Sins (Pride, Envy, Anger, Sloth, Covetousness, Gluttony, Lust) and to amplify all aspects of the Seven Virtues - the three Theological Virtues (Faith, Hope, Love/Charity) and the four Cardinal Virtues (Prudence, Justice, Fortitude, Temperance).

For each of the Seven Visits, there are meditations based on the number seven found in our Catholic Faith. A summary of the Visit and the meditation considerations are described below.

	Deadly Sins	Theological and Cardinal Virtues	Meditation Considerations
Visit One	Pride	Faith	Seven Days of Creation
Visit Two	Envy	Justice	Seven Beatitudes
Visit Three	Anger	Courage	Seven Last Words of Christ on the Cross
Visit Four	Sloth	Prudence	Seven Times Jesus said "I AM"
Visit Five	Covetousness	Temperance	Seven Sorrows of the Blessed Virgin Mary
Visit Six	Gluttony	Charity	Seven Corporal Works of Mercy
Visit Seven	Lust	Hope	Seven Sacraments

Dante's <u>Divine Comedy</u> is organized on the basis of the number seven - the seven circles of *Inferno;* the seven terraces on the mountain of *Purgatorio*; and, the seven spheres of *Paradiso*. Three pictures from <u>The Doré Illustrations for Dante's Divine Comedy</u> are included for each of the Seven Visits. The first picture is from *Purgatorio* and reflects on the particular vice we wish to eliminate. The next two pictures are from *Paradiso* with the celestial pictures giving us one artist's interpretation of the beatific vision - God's promise of eternal life.

Between each of the Sacred Scripture meditations, a couplet litany invokes Jesus' and Mary's help and support during our time of prayer, meditation, and contemplation. For those who wish to use this prayer book in an ecclesiastical setting, we provide musical scores for this couplet litany. This music was written by award-winning composer and singer, Nancy Scimone.

We pray that this book of meditations will open your heart to spend more time in Eucharistic Adoration. Jesus is our friend, and our love, should we not spend some part of our day with Him and His Blessed Mother?

Christine Haapala

May 29th, 2005
Feast of Corpus Christi

IN HIS PRESENCE
Seven Visits to the Blessed Sacrament

The promises of the LORD are sure, / silver refined in a
crucible, / silver purified seven times. ... On each of the
seven days you shall offer an oblation to the LORD. ...
Seven times a day I praise you / because your edicts are just.
Ps 12:7, Lv 23:8, Ps 119:164

THE PRIDEFUL - ODERISI
ABREAST, like oxen going in a yoke, /
I with that heavy-laden soul went on…
(Purgatorio XII, 1-2)

VISIT ONE
Seven Days of Creation

Let us pray for a decrease in our sins of Pride.
Let us pray for an increase in the virtue of Faith
by contemplating the mystery of Creation — the
work of God's Hand — in light of Jesus Christ, the
Crucified, Risen One.

The beginning of pride is man's stubbornness / in withdrawing his heart from his Maker. *Sir 10:12*

Our Father... Hail Mary... Glory to the Father...

In the beginning, when God created the heavens and the earth ... God said, "Let there be light." ... In the beginning was the Word, / and the Word was with God ... For God so loved the world that he gave his only Son... ... Everyone who believes that Jesus is the Christ is begotten by God. *Gn 1:1,3, Jn 1:1, Jn 3:16, 1 Jn 5:1*

One God, Holy Trinity, have mercy on us.
Hail Mary, conceived without sin, pray for us.

God made the dome, and it separated the water above the dome from the water below it. ... "Everyone who drinks this water will be thirsty again; but whoever drinks the water I shall give will never thirst; the water I shall give will become in him a spring of water welling up to eternal life." *Gn 1:7, Jn 4:13-14*

One God, Holy Trinity, have mercy on us.
Hail Mary, conceived without sin, pray for us.

3

God called the dry land "the earth," and basin of the water he called "the sea." ... [H]e got up, rebuked the winds and the sea, and there was great calm. The men were amazed and said, "What sort of man is this, whom even the winds and the seas obey?" *Gn 1:10, Mt 8:26-27*

> *One God, Holy Trinity, have mercy on us.*
> *Hail Mary, conceived without sin, pray for us.*

[T]he sky proclaims its builder's craft. / One day to the next. ... God said: "Let there be lights in the dome of the sky, to separate day from night." ... "I came into the world as light, so that everyone who believes in me might not remain in darkness." ... "I, Jesus, ... am ... the bright morning star." *Ps 19:2-3, Gn 1:14, Jn 12:46, Rv 22:16*

> *One God, Holy Trinity, have mercy on us.*
> *Hail Mary, conceived without sin, pray for us.*

God created the great sea monsters and all kinds of swimming creatures with which the water teems, and all kinds of winged birds. ... Praise the LORD from the earth, / you sea monsters and all deep waters. ... [T]hey saw Jesus walking on the sea and coming near the boat, and they began to be afraid. *Gn 1:21, Ps 148:7, Jn 6:19*

> *One God, Holy Trinity, have mercy on us.*
> *Hail Mary, conceived without sin, pray for us.*

MERCURY

So I beheld more than a thousand splendours /
Drawing towards us, and in each was heard. /
Lo, this is she who shall increase our love.
(Paradiso V, 103-105)

God created man in his own image; / in the divine image he created him; / male and female he created them. ... He is the image of the invisible God, / the firstborn of all creation. / For in him were created all things in heaven and on earth. ... For through faith you are all children of God in Christ Jesus. *Gn 1:27, Col 1:15-16, Gal 3:26*

One God, Holy Trinity, have mercy on us.
Hail Mary, conceived without sin, pray for us.

God ... rested on the seventh day from all the work. ... God blessed the seventh day and made it holy ... a day for sacred assembly. ... "I am the resurrection and the life; whoever believes in me ... will never die. Do you believe this?" ... "Heaven and earth will pass away, but my words will not pass away." *Gn 2:2-3, Lv 23:3, Jn 11:25-26, Lk 21:33*

One God, Holy Trinity, have mercy on us.
Hail Mary, conceived without sin, pray for us.

THE SUN - GLORIFIED SOULS
In such wise of those sempiternal roses /
The garlands twain encompassed us about, /
And thus the outer to the inner answered.
(Paradiso XII, 19-21)

THE ENVIOUS
Covered with sackcloth vile they seemed to me, /
And one sustained the other with his shoulder, /
And all of them were by the bank sustained.
(Purgatorio XIII, 58-60)

Visit Two
Seven Beatitudes

Let us pray for a decrease in our sins of Envy. Let us pray for an increase in the virtue of Justice by living the message of the beatitudes illuminated by the mercy of Jesus' healing hand.

But by the envy of the devil, death entered the world. … Whoever sins belongs to the devil, because the devil has sinned from the beginning. ... For the wages of sin is death... *Wis 2:24, 1 Jn 3:8, Rom 6:23*

Our Father… Hail Mary… Glory to the Father…

"Blessed are the poor in spirit, / for theirs is the kingdom of heaven." … Better the poverty of the just. … "[T]his poor widow put in more than all the rest; … she, from her poverty." … Did not God choose those who are poor in the world to be … heirs of the kingdom? *Mt 5:3, Ps 37:16, Lk 21:3-4, Jas 2:5*

Just Judge, Merciful King, have mercy on us.
Holy Queen, Mother of Mercy, pray for us.

"Blessed are they who mourn, / for they will be comforted." … In the path of justice there is life. … When the Lord saw [the widow], he was moved with pity for her. … [Jesus] stepped forward and touched the coffin … The dead man sat up … and Jesus gave him to his mother. *Mt 5:4, Prv 12:28, Lk 7:13-15*

Just Judge, Merciful King, have mercy on us.
Holy Queen, Mother of Mercy, pray for us.

9

For the LORD is a God of justice: / blessed are all who wait for him! ... "Blessed are the meek, / for they will inherit the land." ... Simon's mother-in-law lay sick with fever. ... He approached, grasped her hand, and helped her up. Then the fever left her and she waited on them. *Is 30:18, Mt 5:5, Mk 1:30-31*

Just Judge, Merciful King, have mercy on us.
Holy Queen, Mother of Mercy, pray for us.

"Blessed are they who hunger and thirst for righteousness, / for they will be satisfied." ... But even if you should suffer because of righteousness, blessed are you. ... "I am the bread of life; whoever comes to me will never hunger, and whoever believes in me will never thirst." *Mt 5:6, 1Pt 3:14, Jn 6:35*

Just Judge, Merciful King, have mercy on us.
Holy Queen, Mother of Mercy, pray for us.

"Blessed are the merciful, / for they will be shown mercy." ... "Do you see this woman? When I entered your house, you did not give me water for my feet, but she has bathed them with her tears ... she anointed my feet with ointment. ... [S]he has shown great love." *Mt 5:7, Lk 7:44, 46-47*

Just Judge, Merciful King, have mercy on us.
Holy Queen, Mother of Mercy, pray for us.

MARS
Well was I ware that I was more uplifted /
By the enkindled smiling of the star, /
That seemed to me more ruddy than its wont.
(Paradiso XIV, 85-87)

"Blessed are the clean of heart, / for they will see God."
[Jesus] said to her, "... The demon has gone out of your
daughter." When the woman went home, she found the child
lying in bed and the demon gone. ... [T]he souls of the just
are in the hand of God, / and no torment shall touch them.
Mt 5:8, Mk 7:29-30, Wis 3:1

> *Just Judge, Merciful King, have mercy on us.*
> *Holy Queen, Mother of Mercy, pray for us.*

"Blessed are the peacemakers, / for they will be called
children of God." ... Then children were brought to him
that he might lay his hands on them and pray. ... Jesus said,
"Let the children come to me, ... for the kingdom of heaven
belongs to such as these." *Mt 5:9, Mt 19:13-14*

> *Just Judge, Merciful King, have mercy on us.*
> *Holy Queen, Mother of Mercy, pray for us.*

JUPITER
So from within those lights the holy creatures /
Sang flying to and fro…
(Paradiso XVIII, 76-77)

THE STONING OF STEPHEN
Then saw I people hot in fire of wrath, /
With stones a young man slaying, clamorously /
Still crying to each other, Kill him! kill him!
(Purgatorio XV, 106-108)

VISIT THREE
Seven Last Words of Christ on the Cross

Let us pray for a decrease in our sins of Anger. Let us pray for an increase in the virtue of Courage by contemplating Jesus' Last Words and joining His Mother at the foot of His cross.

Woe to him who builds a city by bloodshed. ... [D]o not let the sun set on your anger, and do not leave room for the devil ... for seven abominations are in his heart. *Hb 2:12, Eph 4:26-27, Prv 26:25*

Our Father... Hail Mary... Glory to the Father...

"And if he wrongs you seven times in one day and returns to you seven times saying 'I am sorry,' you should forgive him." ... Jesus said, "Father, forgive them, they know not what they do." *Lk 17:4, Lk 23:34*

*Lamb of God, obedient unto death, have mercy on us.
Most pure, Mother of our Savior, pray for us.*

One dies in full vigor, / wholly at ease / ... Another dies in bitterness of soul, / ... Alike they lie down in the dust. ... "Amen, I say to you, today you will be with me in Paradise." ... "I tell you, there will be rejoicing among the angels of God over one sinner who repents." *Job 21:23,25-26, Lk 23:43, Lk 15:10*

*Lamb of God, obedient unto death, have mercy on us.
Most pure, Mother of our Savior, pray for us.*

15

Do not stay far from me, / for trouble is near, / and there is no one to help. ... And at three o'clock Jesus cried out in a loud voice, "Eloi, Eloi, lema sabachthani? ... My God, my God, why have you forsaken me?" ... Even when I cry out for help, / he stops my prayer. *Ps 22:12, Mk 15:34, Lam 3:8*

Lamb of God, obedient unto death, have mercy on us.
Most pure, Mother of our Savior, pray for us.

I went about in grief ... / bent in mourning as for my mother. ... As a mother comforts her son, / so will I comfort you; / in Jerusalem you shall find your comfort. ... "Woman, behold, your son." ... "Behold, your mother." ... Indeed we call blessed those who have persevered. *Ps 35:14, Is 66:13, Jn 19:26-27, Jas 5:11*

Lamb of God, obedient unto death, have mercy on us.
Most pure, Mother of our Savior, pray for us.

O God, ... / For you my body yearns; / for you my soul thirsts, / Like a land parched, lifeless, / and without water. ... "I thirst." ... I am in distress; / with grief my eyes are wasted, / my soul and body spent. ... "Lord Jesus, receive my spirit. ... Lord, do not hold this sin against them." *Ps 63:2, Jn 19:28, Ps 31:10, Acts 7:59-60*

Lamb of God, obedient unto death, have mercy on us.
Most pure, Mother of our Savior, pray for us.

JUPITER
O soldiery of heaven, whom I contemplate, /
Implore for those who are upon the earth /
All gone astray after the bad example! /
(Paradiso XVIII, 124-126)

"Consecrate to me every first-born..." ... Son though he was, he learned obedience from what he suffered ... [and] became the source of eternal salvation for all who obey him. ... "It is finished."... For our paschal lamb, Christ, has been sacrificed. *Ex 13:2, Heb 5:8-9, Jn 19:30, 1 Cor 5:7*

Lamb of God, obedient unto death, have mercy on us.
Most pure, Mother of our Savior, pray for us.

"Father, into your hands I commend my spirit." ... "Worthy is the Lamb that was slain / to receive power and riches, wisdom and strength." ... "Salvation comes from our God, who is seated on the throne, / and from the Lamb." ... "Alleluia! / Salvation, glory, and might belong to our God." *Lk 23:46, Rv 5:12, Rv 7:10, Rv 19:1*

Lamb of God, obedient unto death, have mercy on us.
Most pure, Mother of our Savior, pray for us.

THE CROSS
Here doth my memory overcome my genius; /
For on that cross as levin gleamed forth Christ, /
So that I cannot find ensample worthy…
(Paradiso XIV, 103-105)

THE SLOTHFUL

But taken from me was this drowsiness /
Suddenly by a people, that behind /
Our backs already had come round to us.
(Purgatorio XVIII, 88-90)

VISIT FOUR
Seven Times Jesus said "I AM"

Let us pray for a decrease in our sins of Sloth. Let us pray for an increase in the virtue of Prudence by contemplating the majesty of Christ – He is the GREAT I AM.

[H]old fast to your duty, busy yourself with it, / grow old while doing your task. ... Work at your tasks in due season, / and in his own time God will give you your reward. *Sir 11:20, Sir 51:30*

Our Father... Hail Mary... Glory to the Father...

The woman said to him, "I know that the Messiah is coming, the one called the Anointed; when he comes, he will tell us everything." Jesus said to her, "I am he..." ... "Believe me that I am in the Father and the Father is in me, or else, believe because of the works." *Jn 4:25-26, Jn 14:11*

Holy One, Incarnate Word, have mercy on us.
Virgin Blest, Ark of the Covenant, pray for us.

[T]hey saw Jesus walking on the sea and coming near the boat, and they began to be afraid. But he said to them, "It is I." ... "Great and wonderful are your works, / Lord God almighty. / Just and true are your ways." *Jn 6:19-20, Rv 15:3*

Holy One, Incarnate Word, have mercy on us.
Virgin Blest, Ark of the Covenant, pray for us.

The Rock – how faultless are his deeds, / how right all his ways! … "You belong to this world, but I do not belong to this world. … For if you do not believe that I AM, you will die in your sins." *Dt 32:4, Jn 8:23-24*

Holy One, Incarnate Word, have mercy on us.
Virgin Blest, Ark of the Covenant, pray for us.

"When you lift up the Son of Man, then you will realize that I AM, and that I do nothing on my own, but I say only what the Father taught me." … "I have given you a model to follow, so that as I have done for you, you should also do." *Jn 8:28, Jn 13:15*

Holy One, Incarnate Word, have mercy on us.
Virgin Blest, Ark of the Covenant, pray for us.

Jesus said to them, "Amen, amen, I say to you, before Abraham came to be, I AM." So they picked up stones to throw at him. … The Jews again picked up rocks to stone him. Jesus answered them, "I have shown you many good works from my Father. For which of these are you trying to stone me?" *Jn 8:58-59, Jn 10:31-32*

Holy One, Incarnate Word, have mercy on us..
Virgin Blest, Ark of the Covenant, pray for us.

THE EAGLE
APPEARED before me with its wings outspread /
The beautiful image that in sweet fruition /
Made jubilant the interwoven souls.
(Paradiso XIX, 1-3)

23

If you see a man of prudence, seek him out; / let your feet wear away his doorstep! ... "From now on I am telling you before it happens, so that when it happens, you may believe that I AM." *Sir 6:36, Jn 13:19*

Holy One, Incarnate Word, have mercy on us.
Virgin Blest, Ark of the Covenant, pray for us.

[Jesus] said to them, "I AM" ... When he said to them "I AM," they turned away and fell to the ground. ... "Whom are you looking for?" They said, "Jesus the Nazorean." Jesus answered, "I told you that I AM." ... Be imitators of me, as I am of Christ. ... They stoned Paul and dragged him out of the city, ... he got up and entered the city. *Jn 18:5-8, 1 Cor 11:1, Acts 14:19-20*

Holy One, Incarnate Word, have mercy on us.
Virgin Blest, Ark of the Covenant, pray for us.

THE EAGLE
Because those living luminaries all, /
By far more luminous, did songs begin /
Lapsing and falling from my memory.
(Paradiso XX, 10-12)

THE AVARICIOUS
Onward we went with footsteps slow and scarce, /
And I attentive to the shades I heard / Piteously weeping and
bemoaning them…
(Purgatorio XX, 16-18)

Visit Five
Seven Sorrows of the Blessed Virgin Mary

Let us pray for a decrease in our sins of Covetousness. Let us pray for an increase in the virtue of Temperance by contemplating the Seven Sorrows of the Blessed Virgin Mary.

Direct my heart toward your decrees / and away from unjust gain. / Avert my eyes from what is worthless. *Ps 119:36-37*

Our Father... Hail Mary... Glory to the Father...

For where your treasure is, there also will your heart be. ... Simeon blessed them and said to Mary his mother, "Behold, this child is destined ... to be a sign that will be contradicted (and you yourself a sword will pierce) ... "You shall love the Lord, your God, with all your heart..." *Mt 6:21, Lk 2:34-35, Mt 22:37*

Only Son, Splendor of the Father, have mercy on us.
Immaculate Heart, pierced by a sword, pray for us.

[T]he angel of the Lord appeared to Joseph in a dream and said, "Rise, take the child and his mother, flee to Egypt..." ... How long, LORD? ... / How long must I carry sorrow in my soul, / grief in my heart day after day? ... And Mary kept all these things, reflecting on them in her heart. *Mt 2:13, Ps 13:2-3, Lk 2:19*

Only Son, Splendor of the Father, have mercy on us.
Immaculate Heart, pierced by a sword, pray for us.

[Mary] said to him, "Son, why have you done this to us? Your father and I have been looking for you with great anxiety." … Cease your cries of mourning, / wipe the tears from your eyes. / The sorrow you have shown shall have its reward, / says the LORD! *Lk 2:48, Jer 31:16*

Only Son, Splendor of the Father, have mercy on us.
Immaculate Heart, pierced by a sword, pray for us.

A large crowd of people followed Jesus, including many women who mourned and lamented him. … "Come, all you who pass by the way, / look and see / Whether there is any suffering like my suffering…" … I will see you again, and your hearts will rejoice, and no one will take your joy away from you. *Lk 23:27, Lam 1:12, Jn 16:22*

Only Son, Splendor of the Father, have mercy on us.
Immaculate Heart, pierced by a sword, pray for us.

Why do you let me see ruin; / why must I look at misery? … For whoever does the will of my heavenly Father is … my mother. … Standing by the cross of Jesus were his mother… and the disciple there whom he loved … doing the will of God from the heart, willingly serving the Lord… *Hb 1:3, Mt 12:50, Jn 19:25, Eph 6:6-7*

Only Son, Splendor of the Father, have mercy on us.
Immaculate Heart, pierced by a sword, pray for us.

SATURN
A stairway I beheld to such a height /
Uplifted, that mine eye pursued it not.
(Paradiso XXI, 29-30)

Taking the body, Joseph wrapped it [in] clean linen and laid it in his new tomb that he had hewn in the rock. ... I will turn their mourning into joy, / I will console and gladden them after their sorrows. *Mt 27:59-60, Jer 31:13*

Only Son, Splendor of the Father, have mercy on us.
Immaculate Heart, pierced by a sword, pray for us.

Out of six troubles he will deliver you, / and at the seventh no evil shall touch you. ... [W]hen they had seen the tomb and the way in which his body was laid in it, [the women] returned and prepared spices and perfumed oils. ... "Arise, LORD, come to your resting place, / you and your majestic ark." *Job 5:19, Lk 23:55-56, Ps 132:8*

Only Son, Splendor of the Father, have mercy on us.
Immaculate Heart, pierced by a sword, pray for us.

THE QUEEN OF HEAVEN
"Thou shalt behold enthroned the Queen /
To whom this realm is subject and devoted."
(Paradiso XXXI, 116-117)

THE GLUTTONS
And shadows, that appeared things doubly dead, /
From out the sepulchres of their eyes betrayed /
Wonder at me, aware that I was living.
(Purgatorio XXIV, 4-6)

Visit Six
Seven Corporal Works of Mercy

Let us pray for a decrease in our sins of Gluttony. Let us pray for an increase in the virtue of Charity by imitating Christ through the Seven Corporal Works of Mercy.

Court not death by your erring way of life. ... [L]ive soberly ... do not act in compliance with the desires of your former ignorance but, as he who called you is holy, be holy yourselves. *Wis 1:12, 1 Pt 1:13-15*

Our Father... Hail Mary... Glory to the Father...

The maker of heaven and earth / ... gives food to the hungry. ... God rained manna upon them for food; / bread from heaven he gave them. ... Jesus took the loaves, gave thanks, and distributed them. ... "I am the bread of life; whoever comes to me will never hunger." *Ps 146:6-7, Ps 78:24, Jn 6:11, Jn 6:35*

Jesus, Model of all Virtues, have mercy on us.
Our Lady, Help of Christians, pray for us.

If your enemy be ... / thirsty, give him to drink. ... [God] split rock in the desert, / gave water ... / rivers of water. ... "I am the bread of life; whoever comes to me ... will never thirst." ... With joy you will draw water / at the fountain of salvation. *Prv 25:21, Ps 78:15-16, Jn 6:35, Is 12:3*

Jesus, Model of all Virtues, have mercy on us.
Our Lady, Help of Christians, pray for us.

If a brother or sister has nothing to wear ... but you do not give them the necessities of the body, what good is it? ... If a man is virtuous – if he does what is right and just, ... if he ... clothes the naked; ... he shall surely live, says the Lord GOD. ... For I was ... naked .... whatever you did for one of these least brothers of mine, you did for me. *Jas 2:15-16, Ez 18:5,7,9, Mt 25:35-36,40*

> *Jesus, Model of all Virtues, have mercy on us.*
> *Our Lady, Help of Christians, pray for us.*

[The Samaritan] lifted him up on his own animal, took him to an inn and cared for him. ... I say, love your enemies, do good to those who hate you. ... Love your enemies and do good to them, and lend expecting nothing back. *Lk 10:34, Lk 6:27, Lk 6:35*

> *Jesus, Model of all Virtues, have mercy on us.*
> *Our Lady, Help of Christians, pray for us.*

Do not be afraid of anything that you are going to suffer. Indeed, the devil will throw some of you into prison. ... For I was ... in prison and you visited me. ... Peter thus was being kept in prison, but prayer by the church was fervently being made to God on his behalf. ... Lead me out of my prison, / that I may give thanks to your name. *Rv 2:10, Mt 25:35-36, Acts 12:5, Ps 142:8*

> *Jesus, Model of all Virtues, have mercy on us.*
> *Our Lady, Help of Christians, pray for us.*

THE HEAVEN OF THE FIXED STARS
"GLORY be to the Father, to the Son, /
And Holy Ghost !" all Paradise began, /
So that the melody inebriate made me.
(Paradiso XXVII, 1-3)

"God has visited his people." ... "Go and tell John what you have seen and heard: the blind regain their sight, the lame walk, lepers are cleansed, the deaf hear." ... A large number of people ... gathered, bringing the sick and those disturbed by unclean spirits, and they were all cured. *Lk 7:16, Lk 7:22, Acts 5:16*

Jesus, Model of all Virtues, have mercy on us.
Our Lady, Help of Christians, pray for us.

"She has done a good thing for me. ... She has done what she could. She has anticipated anointing my body for burial." ... Weep over the dead man, for his light has gone out; / ... Weep but a little over the dead man, for he is at rest; / ... Seven days of mourning for the dead... *Mk 14:6,8, Sir 22:9-11*

Jesus, Model of all Virtues, have mercy on us.
Our Lady, Help of Christians, pray for us.

CRYSTALLINE HEAVEN
Not otherwise does iron scintillate /
When molten, than those circles scintillated.
(Paradiso, XXVIII, 89-90)

THE SEVENTH CIRCLE - THE LUSTFUL
And spirits saw I walking through the flame; /
Wherefore I looked, to my own steps and theirs /
Apportioning my sight from time to time.
(Purgatorio XXV, 124-126)

VISIT SEVEN
Seven Sacraments

Let us pray for a decrease in our sins of Lust. Let us pray for an increase in the virtue of Hope by living the Catholic Sacramental life in the hope of eternal life.

"In [the] last time there will be scoffers who will live according to their own godless desires." ... [K]eep away from worldly desires that wage war against the soul. *Jude 18, 1Pt 2:11*

Our Father... Hail Mary... Glory to the Father...

"This is my beloved Son..." ... one Lord, one faith, one baptism; one God and Father of all. ... "Go, therefore, and make disciples of all nations, baptizing them in the name of the Father, and of the Son, and of the holy Spirit." ... I will sprinkle clean water upon you to cleanse you from all your impurities. *Mt 3:17, Eph 4:5-6, Mt 28:19, Ez 36:25*

Word made Flesh, Divine Eucharist, have mercy on us. Lady of Hope, Gate of Heaven, pray for us.

"O God, be merciful to me a sinner." ... [M]any tax collectors and sinners came and sat with Jesus. ... "I desire mercy ... I did not come to call the righteous but sinners." ... "Whose sins you forgive are forgiven them, and whose sins you retain are retained." *Lk 18:13, Mt 9:10,13, Jn 20:23*

Word made Flesh, Divine Eucharist, have mercy on us. Lady of Hope, Gate of Heaven, pray for us.

On the first day of the Feast of Unleavened Bread, ... [Jesus] took his place at table with the apostles. ... The cup of blessing that we bless, is it not a participation in the blood of Christ? The bread that we break, is it not a participation in the body of Christ? ... "Whoever eats my flesh and drinks my blood has eternal life." *Mt 26:17, Lk 22:14, 1 Cor 10:16, Jn 6:54*

Word made Flesh, Divine Eucharist, have mercy on us.
Lady of Hope, Gate of Heaven, pray for us.

"I am sending the promise of my Father upon you; but stay in the city until you are clothed with power from on high." ... Then there appeared to them tongues as of fire, which parted and came to rest on each one of them. And they were all filled with the holy Spirit. ... God, your God, has anointed you / with the oil of gladness. *Lk 24:49, Acts 2:3-4, Ps 45:8*

Word made Flesh, Divine Eucharist, have mercy on us.
Lady of Hope, Gate of Heaven, pray for us.

This is a great [sacrament] ... each one of you should love his wife as himself, and the wife should respect her husband. ... I will espouse you to me forever: / I will espouse you ... / in love and in mercy; / I will espouse you in fidelity, / and you shall know the LORD. *Eph 5:32-33, Hos 2:21-22*

Word made Flesh, Divine Eucharist, have mercy on us.
Lady of Hope, Gate of Heaven, pray for us.

THE EMPYREAN

In fashion then as of a snow-white rose /
Displayed itself to me the saintly host, /
Whom Christ in his own blood had made his bride.
(Paradiso, XXXI, 1-3)

Christ came as high priest ... entered once for all into the sanctuary ... with his own blood, thus obtaining eternal redemption. ... "It was not you who chose me, but I who chose you." ..."You are a priest forever." ... "This is my body, which will be given for you; do this in memory of me." *Heb 9:11-12, Jn 15:16, Heb 7:17, Lk 22:19*

Word made Flesh, Divine Eucharist, have mercy on us.
Lady of Hope, Gate of Heaven, pray for us.

So they went off and preached repentance ... [and] anointed with oil many who were sick and cured them. ... How great the mercy of the LORD, / his forgiveness of those who return to him! ... For you are [dust], / and to [dust] you shall return. *Mk 6:12-13, Sir 17:24, Gn 3:19*

Word made Flesh, Divine Eucharist, have mercy on us.
Lady of Hope, Gate of Heaven, pray for us.

THE HEAVEN OF THE FIXED STARS
Begin then, and declare to what thy soul /
Is aimed, and count it for a certainty, /
Sight is in thee bewildered and not dead…
(Paradiso, XXVI, 7-9)

43

Musical Scores for
Couplet Litany Invocations

Visit One
Seven Days of Creation

One God, Ho-ly Tri - ni - ty, have mer - cy on us, have mer - cy on us.

Hail Ma - ry, con-ceived with-out sin, pray for us, pray for us.

Visit Two
Seven Beatitudes

Just Judge, Mer - ci - ful King, have mer - cy on us, have mer - cy on us.

Ho - ly Queen, Mo - ther of Mer-cy, pray for us, pray for us.

Visit Three
Seven Last Words of Christ on the Cross

Lamb of God, o-bed-ient un-to death, have mer - cy on us, have mer - cy on us.

Most pure, Mo-ther of our Sav-ior, pray for us, pray for us.

VISIT FOUR
Seven Times Jesus said "I AM"

Ho - ly One, In - car - nate Word, have mer - cy on us, have mer - cy on us.

Vir - gin Blest, Ark of the Cov-e-nant, pray for us, pray for us.

VISIT FIVE
Seven Sorrows of the Blessed Virgin Mary

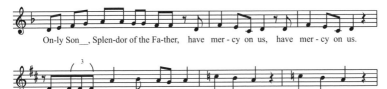

On-ly Son__, Splen-dor of the Fa-ther, have mer - cy on us, have mer - cy on us.

Im - mac-u-late Heart, pierced by a sword, pray for us, pray for us.

VISIT SIX
Seven Corporal Works of Mercy

Je - sus, Mo - del of all Vir - tues, have mer - cy on us, have mer - cy on us.

Our La - dy, Help of___ Chris-tians, pray for us, pray for us.

VISIT SEVEN
Seven Sacraments

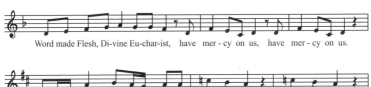

Word made Flesh, Di-vine Eu-char-ist, have mer - cy on us, have mer - cy on us.

La - dy of Hope, Gate of ___ Hea-ven, pray for us, pray for us.

THE PRAYERS

OUR FATHER

Our Father, Who art in Heaven, hallowed be Thy Name. Thy kingdom come, Thy will be done on earth as it is in Heaven. Give us this day our daily bread, and forgive us our trespasses, as we forgive those who trespass against us. And lead us not into temptation, but deliver us from evil. Amen.

HAIL MARY

Hail Mary, full of grace, the Lord is with thee; blessed art thou among women, and blessed is the Fruit of thy womb, Jesus. Holy Mary, Mother of God, pray for us sinners, now and at the hour of our death.
Amen.

GLORY TO THE FATHER

Glory to the Father, and to the Son, and to the Holy Spirit: as it was in the beginning, is now, and will be for ever.
Amen.

Products from Suffering Servant Scriptorium

PRAYER BOOKS FOR CHILDREN OF ALL AGES

<u>Speak, Lord, I am Listening</u> A Rosary Book (2nd Ed, with Luminous Mysteries. Includes Study and Discussion Guide) This prayer book presents the richness of the Sacred Mysteries of the Most Holy Rosary in terms that children can visualize and understand. Gus Muller's watercolors use the full palette of color expression to explore the depths of the agony of Christ crucified and reach the heights of the Blessed Virgin Mary's glorious reign as Queen of Heaven and Earth. Succinct and most apt meditation selections yield a wealth of spiritual insight into the mysterious events of the lives of Jesus and Mary. The Scriptures and watercolor illustrations coupled with the prayers of the Most Holy Rosary provide a rich meditation platform for teaching prayer and devotion to Jesus and Mary.

<u>Follow Me</u> A Stations of the Cross Book. Inspired watercolors and selections of God's Word introduce children to the suffering of our Savior Jesus Christ by walking each step with Him to Calvary. Along with each station is a heroically holy person who epitomized self-sacrifice and was beatified or canonized by Pope John Paul II.

PRAYER BOOKS FOR ADULTS AND TEENAGERS

<u>Seraphim and Cherubim</u> A Scriptural Chaplet of the Holy Angels. Angels have been with us since the beginning in the "Garden of Eden" and will be with us at the "End of Age." This prayer book joins together Sacred Scripture selections with special invocations to our Blessed Mother and the Holy Archangels. This book includes fabulous full-color pictures from the masters, such as, Raphael, Bruegel the Elder, Pe-

rugino and many others. It also includes a newly composed Novena of the Holy Angels and the traditional Litany of the Holy Angels. Those who pray without ceasing and ponder the Good News will find this book equally inspiring and encouraging.

Psalter of Jesus and Mary This pocket-size Scriptural Rosary prayer book includes the 150 Psalms Scriptural Rosary for the Joyful, Sorrowful and Glorious Mysteries and meditations for the Luminous Mysteries from the Book of Proverbs, the wise words of Solomon. The 20 Mysteries of the Most Holy Rosary open with a New Testament reflection. There is a short Scripture meditation from either Psalms or Proverbs for each Hail Mary. An Old and New Testament icon from Julius Schnorr von Carolsfeld's Treasurey of Bible Illustrations accompany each mystery.

His Sorrowful Passion This prayer book integrates Sacred Scripture meditations with the prayers of the Chaplet of Divine Mercy. There are two Scriptural Chaplets: one chronicles Jesus' Passion and the other features the Seven Penitential Psalms. The woodcuts of the 15th century Catholic artist, Albrecht Durer, illustrate this book.

The Suffering Servant's Courage (2nd Ed, with Luminous Mysteries) This prayer book integrates poignant Sacred Scripture verses about courage and fortitude, the prayers of the Most Holy Rosary, and illustrations from the inspired artistry of the 19th century Catholic illustrator Gustave Dore.

From Genesis to Revelation: Seven Scriptural Rosaries This prayer book is the most thorough and extensive collection of Scriptural Rosaries you will find anywhere. This prayer book goes well beyond the traditional Scriptural Rosary and penetrates the heart of the meditative spirit of the mysteries. It addresses many dimensions: time, from the Old to the New Testament; authors, from Moses, Isaiah, to the Evangelists; and perspectives, form the purely historical to deeper spiritual and prayerful insights. Those who pray the Rosary and those who read the Bible will equally find this prayer book inspirational.

RECORDED PRAYERS AVAILABLE ON CD

The Sanctity of Life Scriptural Rosary (2nd Ed. with Luminous Mysteries) Sacred Scripture selections prayed with the Most Holy Rosary uniquely brings you God's message of the dignity and sanctity of life. The prayers are accompanied by meditative piano music. Four different readers lead you in more than two hours of prayerful meditations. Includes four songs from the composer and soprano Nancy Scimone, winner of the UNITY Awards 2002 Best Sacramental Album of the Year for ORA PRO NOBIS. Includes 16-page book with the complete text of the Sacred Scripture selections. Double CD. CD 1 includes the Joyful and Luminous Mysteries and CD 2 includes the Sorrowful and Glorious Mysteries.

Time for Mercy Composer and singer Nancy Scimone offers you a new, spiritually uplifting Chaplet of Divine Mercy melody. This Scriptural Chaplet of Divine Mercy is based on the Penitential Psalm Scriptural Chaplet of Divine Mercy from the book, His Sorrowful Passion. Brother Leonard Konopka, MIC, prays selections from the Seven Penitential Psalms, while Nancy Scimone's crystal clear soprano voice brings us God's message of Divine Mercy.

51

Quantity orders of Suffering Servant Scriptorium books or CDs may be purchased for liturgical, educational, or sale promotional use. For discount schedule and further information, please call toll free 888-652-9494 or write to us at:

Suffering Servant Scriptorium
Special Market Department
PO Box 1126
Springfield, VA 22151